TEN THOUSAND STEPS
AGAINST THE TYRANT

Also by Indran Amirthanayagam

Books

The Elephants of Reckoning, Hanging Loose Press, New York, 1993
Ceylon R.I.P., Institute for Ethnic Studies, Colombo, Sri Lanka 2001
El infierno de los pájaros, Resistencia, Mexico City, Mexico, 2001
El hombre que recoge nidos, Resistencia/Conarte, Monterrey, Mexico, 2005
The Splintered Face (Tsunami Poems), Hanging Loose Press, New York 2008
Sol Camuflado, Lustra Editores, Lima, 2010
La pelota del pulpo (The Octopus's Ball), Editorial Apogeo, Lima, 2012
Sin adorno—lírica para tiempos neobarrocos, Univ. Aut. de N. L., Mexico 2012
Uncivil War, Tsar (now Mawenzi House), Toronto, 2013
Aller-Retour Au Bord de la Mer, Legs Editions, Haiti. 2014
Ventana Azul, El Tapiz del Unicornio, Mexico, 2016
Pwezi a Kat Men (written with Alex LaGuerre). Edition Delince, 2017
Il n'est de solitude que l'île lointaine, Legs Editions, Haiti, 2017
Coconuts On Mars, Poetrywala, Paperwall Publishers, Mumbai, India, 2019
En busca de posada, Editorial Apogeo, Lima, Peru, 2019
Paolo 9, Manofalsa, Lima, Peru, 2019
The Migrant States, Hanging Loose Press, New York, 2020
Lírica, a tiempo, Mesa Redonda, Lima, 2020
Sur l'île nostalgique, L'Harmattan, Paris, 2020
Blue Window (Ventana Azul), translated by Jennifer Rathbun, Dialogos Books, 2021

Music

Rankont Dout, with Donaldzie Theodore, Pawol Tanbou, Titi Congo. Port Au Prince. October 2017
They Died Not in Vain, music video, with Evans Okan, Cuernavaca, November 2019

Ten Thousand Steps Against the Tyrant

Poems

Indran Amirthanayagam

Broadstone

Library of Congress Control Number 2021951330

ISBN 978-1-937968-98-4

Design by Larry W. Moore
Cover Artwork by Anandan Mirae Guyomar,
used by permission

Some of these poems first appeared in the following journals and books:
E-Verse Radio, *The New Verse News*, *The Poetry Channel* on youtube,
Live Encounters, *The Blue Nib*, & *Sur l'île nostalgique*.

Broadstone Books
An Imprint of
Broadstone Media LLC
418 Ann Street
Frankfort, KY 40601-1929
BroadstoneBooks.com

These poems, born in the crucible, mixed with great hope and sometime fear, out of faith in the founding principles, in the idea that one can build a better and more fitting republic, I dedicate to you who inspire these words, your pen rising like a flag, your ears open to the sad music of somebody's child beaten and hungry but at peace now in the new country.

I write these poems for that country, for its better half, its more generous spirit, for its candor and do something know-how, for its kindness to this stranger.

I write these poems for, and from, the beloved who walks with me on the island listening to the monsoon and hurricane, to bird song and heart song, making word music, making poems that sing, exorcising the tyrant.

To Joe and Kamala, to all of us.

Indran Amirthanayagam, November 17, 2021

Contents

(THE MOTHER OF)...PANDEMICS

FOREWORD

As with Walt Whitman's celebratory songs in *Leaves of Grass,* Indran Amirthanayagam's new poetry collection, *Ten Thousand Steps Against the Tyrant,* pays tribute to our country's diversity, optimism, resilience, fortitude, and humanitarian impulses. The book also eloquently laments the needless tragedies spawned by the Trump presidency and era, including the separation of hundreds of immigrant children from their parents, relentless attacks on free speech, widespread joblessness and hunger, climate change, the violent deaths of innocent black men and women, and the Covid-19 pandemic.

Amirthanayagam's poems display a great emotional range, encompassing the joys and sorrows, hopes and fears, anger and tenderness engendered by being an American of conscience living through these tumultuous and uncertain times. As the poet exclaims in "New, New Deal": "We cannot keep quiet when the black man, running from/ a cop, is shot in the back. We cannot allow the future to be snuffed by/ a boot pressed to a man's neck."

Without being pedantic, doctrinaire, nor strident, Amirthanayagam's poems are political in the best possible way, for they act as calls to action on behalf of America's beleaguered and disenfranchised, as well as for the "silent majority" who, in "this once blessed land" are "smarting from / four years of locusts, plague." ("Between Great Fear, Great Hope")

Oracular, bardic, deeply moving and compassionate, the poems in *Ten Thousand Steps Against the Tyrant* implore us to "…remember the neighbor. / Let us take care of each other." ("Love Your Neighbor"). They entreat us to act in solidarity for the good of our fellow citizens, as when the poet slyly claims that "We the people are standing/ back, standing by." ("Morning (Not Mourning) Song") Highly lyrical and expressive, Indran Amirthanayagam's poems are both redemptive and empowering, and they're as personal as they are universal.

This poet's anthem espouses that we Americans, and our treasured democracy, are survivors, and that despite our current suffering, deliverance (like a phoenix rising) is possible: "Mine is a literary reckoning, / preparation of will, ritual suicide. / I will rise again light as ash coating // feathers flapping in the still-glowing air / after the bomb, the virus, the curse / of the orange-haired tyrant." ("Make It Nude") I treasure this book as a testimonial for the year that changed the world forever; it's a 2020 map of despair and hope, a lantern raised in the darkness.

—Maurya Simon

(The Mother of)...Elections

MIGRANT SONG

We need your poems now. We need to hear
the songs of your migrant heart. We need
to understand the meaning of your voyage
throughout the planet, each trip unique,
each trip the prodigal feast. Who are we?
You, me, the neighbor, the friend up the
road, up country, on the other side of the
world. Who are we? Those who believe in
the beautiful, foul, yet saving grace of the
word. Who are we? We sing and boogie.
Move the word through its steps, to the
pulse in our bodies, to the last breath. We
dance the song of Siva, the song of Roland,
the Song of Songs. We carry history on our
backs, in our hearts. We are Tamils and
Armenians, Jews and Palestinians. We are
all people who have moved, who are moving
now, through these migrant states. We write
poems for our tribes, making one tribe of
every beating heart sending blood through
the veins of one earth. We are the first and
the last. And we are singing, dancing,
writing now. We are your friends,
neighbors, unknown, left out. Let us open
our minds and hearts wide. Let us admit all
the migrant states to this feast. Let this feast
become a poem, a pill, that we can eat every
day. Let us say hello, aloha and leave this
party and never say goodbye. Let us meet
again as soon as the word flies, the heart
opens, the bird sings in the morning, the
world wakes up from this pandemic dream
alive and ready to move, to make,
to fill, and to rename the void.

IN LOVE AND POETRY

Call it now. Out loud.
Without shame. By
its name. Call it

this morning on waking
in the still dark. Call it
reading last night

your words on the screen.
Call it banishing sleep.
There is no energy

more sweet that sustains.
Call it for the one
who corrects these verses.

Call it on streets of
suburb and city,
in the fields. Call it

in front of the Capitol
on top of Mount Baldy
on Waikiki Beach,

by Lake Superior.
We are going far my dear
and we are walking back

home for Thanksgiving.
Let us invite Kamala
and Joe to the table.

Let us boil sweet potatoes,
serve elderberry jam,
make a bean and onion stuffing,

let our friends know
the meal will not involve
killing a turkey

or any other fowl.
Let us give thanks God for
this vitamin flowering

in the early dark, guiding
our fingers as we write,
saying call it now,

in the day, at night,
to friends and enemies
alike. In love and poetry

we are going to make
table and bed, and we
are going to write

our songs in these days
of the plague until
we see light come up

above the trees on fire,
the befogged clouds. Until
the back of beyond.

THE RIGHT PATH

Let us roll, America.
Let us not look back.
Let us seize the fellow
by the absent coat-tail.
Let us reveal the traipsing
emperor nude and let us
remember and defend
the rights of our virus
dead, but let us do so
with respect, with love.
Why? Because Jesus
says so. Why? Because
we are not jackals
and hyenas. Why?
Because we have
to get back on the road
to the promised land.

THE RELEVANCE OF ALLEN GINSBERG

I have one more story to share about Allen Ginsberg. I was at Columbia
studying journalism, stressed utterly, with no time for poetry, trying
to get the nut graph right and learning to control my bladder to last
through the news conference and the follow-up interview. Then

I learned that Allen was to feature at a club downtown. Memories
of Honolulu, of our first meeting when he sang Sweet Oahu in the car
playing the harmonium. He told me then to cut half the first draft out.
I could not resist seeing him again so despite the heavy reporting load,

I took the subway down the West Side and walked East. He asked me
if I would read in the Open. I could not refuse. And I read my poem
about the 241 marines bombed in Beirut. And he told me he liked
the tat-a-tat rhymes and story but did not care for the doubting end.

He said you have to take a stance then say it. I am saying it now.
Get rid of the dissembler, hoodlum and pussy-grabber. Get rid of
the thou shalt not enter and the latrine supervisor. Get rid of
the one who would be king. Get rid of the golden tamarind toupee.

Get him out of the people's house. Then speak to me
about the humming birds and next year's cherry blossoms.

ON THE BUS, TOGETHER

What a pleasure you say to take the bus
after so many months of confinement—
masked, Fall light dappling the skin—
stepping out near the White House.

The season, of course, does not
realize the goings-on in that fount
of hopes, ambitions, dreams, or opine
about how to repossess it for the people,

to walk the tyrant out speedily. Not
easy when plans are hatched already
to block access to the bunker, to charge
mayors and governors with

sedition, to send armies of harassers
to polling stations looking for
the shifty, unkempt and fearful
among the people in line to stop

them from casting their ballots. Step
back on that bus before it too is
commissioned. Let us go together
to vote before evening and night fall.

DEEP SONG ANTHEM

We need the deep song.
We are going far and long.
To Pennsylvania Avenue
and beyond. Vote. Donate.

Be strong tonight Kamala.
You will make us proud
on that debate stage
I know. And Joe. Joe

is cooking just fine
And the people are
gathering in the name
of decent government

and truth in speech
and deed. We are
going far and long.
Now Texas is in play

in a serious way.
North Carolina
and the Rust Belt
are coming back

to the fold, Michael Moore,
I salute you.
Congressman Lewis
in your name, and

so many other
brothers and sisters.
Let us remember
Jacob Blake in rehab.

Keep him in prayers.
Keep the families
who have lost
breadwinners,

sons and daughters
to the bullet,
the plague. We
will not forget you.

Morning (not Mourning) Song

Briefing room, White House
infected, press secretary,
deputies infected, but
the chief is flying back
tonight. He is flying
back. Roaches

and larger vermin
are running scared.
Running and crawling
scared. No more crumbs
from journalist pockets.
No more crawfish

from Rose Garden parties.
But the Chief is parachuting,
yes sir, a new valet on call,
a new sergeant-at-arms,
fresh meat, virgin, patriotic,
to greet the flight,

to take a briefcase, a sausage
for the president. The chief
is flying back, deep clean
Secret Service reserves
on duty. It will be
alright. the flight path

set, but not the morning
after. Proud Boys stand
down, eliminate
yourselves into caves.
We the people are
standing back, standing by.

I Can Breathe

"I can't breathe"—George Floyd

A man is gasping for oxygen,
his dream deferred as well.
Proud Boys are crying, Christie,
Hicks, Kellyann Conway
tussling with the unknown sprung

from the unsurprising surprise
October brought to the Rose
Garden, the god-damned virus
floating from mouth to cheek
while150 guests snacked

on jambalaya and crawfish.
The nominee already had
her bout with Covid back
in July. She will survive.
But senators must now

recuse who would
otherwise have crowed
sending her nomination
flying to the floor. And
what about the next

presidential face-off, are
we facing the end
of debates? The Speaker
of the House tests negative
still. My vote is already

at the post office, and
generals will assure
an orderly transition,
this virus leave the garden
in the end so we can go back in

to the new world, yes we can,
wearing fig leaves, wearing
masks through which
we scream the words of
George Floyd's spirit,

saying this time "I can breathe."

Voting Song

I am going to take
Mother to the polling
station. This may be
her last chance to vote

for the right path from
the burning bush,
sinking ship,
road kill, victims

of the raging virus. I
am going to take
Mother to the
polling station.

And Son, make sure
you get that absentee
ballot sent here while
you visit. Every vote

will count. And Daughter,
although you cannot vote,
not this time, I want
you to know

that we have tried
with all of our heart
and mind to throw
the bastards out.

"MY LOVE, I'M VOTING"

I am crying. Yes, but not to worry.
These are happy tears, tears of bliss
I did not think God would have time
to look out for me. Thank you angel
who intervened. Thank you kindness
to strangers, what you taught me
Mum and Dad. Thank you poets.
I love you as I love myself. Thank
you diplomats. Thank you
Kamala and Joe. Thank you friends
of America, Asia, Arabia, Australia,
Europe, India, the Pacific Isles.
Thank you all peoples, animals,
birds, plants, seeds, works of art,
music and dance not yet mentioned.
Thank you my love, voting.

PENCIL

—for Sara

There is a time to mourn and a time
to review the cards and cast them
again on the table trusting God
to guide your hand, to say this pencil
you left with roses, chrysanthemums,
lilies, in a riot of passionate flowers
before the Supreme Court, will be
picked up by a girl after the period
of mourning, not to be conserved
in the Smithsonian's Museum
of American History, but to write
the story of a young lawyer come
to Washington to interpret laws
with grace, acuity and impartiality,
to the best of her ability, until
such time as their articulation
becomes almost unnecessary,
so ingrained they would become
in the social conscience of
Americans walking then freely.

THE RETURN

The pencil is magic—leaving it in offering on steps of the Court, then the call
from the DA's offfice for a second interview. There is a hand beyond, outside,
inside at all times circulating, sweeping up worshippers who have given
the spirit his and her due, who have understood that one knows the world
through heart and head, eyes, breath, and with none of these but learned faith,
trusting the call out of the blue, ready to rise, pick up the phone and recite
the right words, healing words, words that will bring children bawling
and smiling into the world, that will give the wronged the chance to escape
the unjust, that will break down the trickery of the desperate purveyors
of privilege. This is the New Deal again, the throwing out of Coolidge,
Ms. Smith going to Washington, returning now to Paumanok to assure that
Walt Whitman's words will be spoken at this time that Jack Hirschman calls
the American Revolution, to which I add, humbly and in the eyes of God,
the re-revolving rolling raising goose hairs and kissing them without the knife,
this vegetarian, wine-free yet wine-respectful non-American, worldwide electric
spinning dial whirling, whirling from Paumanok to Washington to Frisco Bay,
light as a feather rolling on wind streams into my heart and yours. I too
am walking now and about to run. Do you see me light and hope-filled
grateful that the word is in good hands and coming back to the island
from where it walked abroad, coming back strong?

For the Zoomathon

My shirt is green.
My jeans are blue.
My blood is red.
My eyes are white
in iris, pupil black.
On the 17th poets
of all colors and
without color,
for black lives
that matter,
for all migrants
in our migrant
nation and
for the first
nations who
keep their cultures
alive by the skin of
their teeth
and their long-
toothed wisdom, for
all who have learned
from elders and
history that
we take two steps
forward then fall
one sad step behind
and now we are ready
to make one giant leap
ahead, for all of us.
Great poets, migrant
poets, women poets,
male poets. Poets
of the rainbow, poets
of the sea, poets of
the earth on October 17

5 pm Eastern Standard Time
on Facebook Live
on the LitBalm page
via Zoom. To raise green
for Joe and Kamala and
the Democrats. Come
to your windows. Donate.
Vote. This is Indran
Amirthanayagam
reading with you.

Restoring the Dream

We have soared West from East,
roared to the Plains, jumped back
to support the rising tide, belly fire
of disenfranchised in the South.
This ia a front court, back court full
court press We are not going to
stop, Joe in Ohio, in Little Haiti,
Miami, Kamala everywhere
our hearts open to the historic
child of the immigrant state
flourishing. We are not going
to stop and here is the plan:
first secure 1600 Pennsylvania Avenue.
Give it a deep clean, then do
the same in state houses we claim,
to practice good governance again,
to create jobs again, to assure health
insurance and the chance to study
for all of us. Black lives matter.
Congressman Lewis did not live and die
in vain. We are rolling. We are screaming.
We are singing. We are cooing lullabies.
We are not going to be silent. And with you
Kamala, with you Joe we want to save
our American Dream, make it currency
again for the world to trust, to exchange.
We are going back to Paris to sign that
accord, a first step towards saving the
polar bear and all the other bears.
And you heard it here. George McGovern,
Walter Mondale, Michael Dukakis, Al Gore,
John Kerry, and Hillary Clinton. We
are walking with you, to realize the dreams

left pending. And Jimmy, Bill. Barack.
Thank you for getting the Dream together,
for giving us hope that we could go on.
And now we are going on. We are going strong.

9/11, West

These anniversaries
help carry the load,
every date spilling
blood but some
standing out for
the grandeur of
the offense,
the sweep of evil.
Today, 9/11, is a day
for campaigns to stop
and citizens to pay
respects, family
and friends gathering
round, the exhausted
soul rising despite the
thick, orange-white
smoke.

A Mole for the Side

I wanted to stopper
these feelings like
clogging a drain
scraping the mole
off my forehead
pasting a bandage
on it in private
off camera until
I would come out
like a bear from
hibernation
ravenous eyes
racing but I had
a previous
engagement
via Zoom
a reading which
my diplomatic
public affairs
persona did not
want to refuse.
Now I am
getting
expressions
of alarm
about the mole
and I am writing
this poem conscious
that I must call
Dermatologists Inc.
to request puncturing
or freezing of
the blackening hole
then sweeping it up
before some ill-

disposed cells
decide to rebel
turning against
the union which I
offer you for
richer and poorer,
in sickness and health,
from my migrant state.

Soul Rising

I miss you something fierce;
I have to tell my bones to
stop shaking, to calm
down, that there is something
called work, poetry, cleaning
the room, getting food
together, attending to mother,
reading fine print in polling,
picking up the phone, cold-
calling a Texan in the name of
participatory democracy, the
nation's and the earth's soul,
and the Dream, jostling about
in the coffin thinking the time
is now to break down the
wood, pierce the earth, slide
out to walk abroad again
through these United States.

Address beyond Gettysburg

We are not going to stop. We have already started to walk, to run, our legs
stretching, striding. The wind is behind us blowing our hair and pushing
us ahead. Every day every hour every minute fills us with enormous adrenalin,
enormous hope. There are only so many insults the brain and heart can take
before they begin to fight back, but with guidance, from the village elder,
to dilute the poisoned barb with herbs and prayers to get the Russians
on the back foot, to invite Chinese to return to business, to let ordinary
Iranians drink coffee in peace. But I am not a mere internationalist.
No, my friends I am running with Iowa farmers, former steel workers
of Bethlehem, chicken pickers of Perdue plants in Tennessee.
I am not satisfied with the way things are in fifty states and all
the dependencies. In Puerto Rico I will not ignore people after
they suffer hurricanes twice. In New Orleans, and the Bayou,
I am not going to stop at building a levee. I will build parishes
back with the faith that sustains me and them, that we will see
a promised land, that we can arrive there together, one nation
under God. And I have only just begun. Just begun. Give me
your stories from every community, every state house.
We are going to talk among ourselves, one great family
conversation around the fireplace, the TV, the radio,
the computer, the phone. We are going to go back
towards building that Great Society. Do you remember
the dream deferred? Langston Hughes will be on my night table.
Congressman Lewis will dance in my dreams as he did
in Congress. Blue Dog democrats will have their say
at the table. And we will listen to reasonable arguments
from the other aisle. What is reasonable? That we spend
the budget to get people back to work, in good health
and with hope; that we make peace with our friends
again, and we trust but verify our enemies.

On Denial of Listing
the Poets' Political Fundraiser

Respectfully I disagree. All events
are political—Greek root polis,
community...community matter.
But in the interest of consensus
I will walk away from the zoom
room when this vote is called.
Let the Translation newsletter
go to press without mention of
the several translator poets
from various languages who
will read for the cause, without
a thousand flowers blooming.

POET AND CITIZEN

The Zoomathon readings have a litmus test—
despite my internationalist credentials, belief
in open borders, free flow of people and ideas—
I will admit the poems have to strum chords
in the deepest song of the heart and they need
to be written by American citizens. Politics
remains a local matter, one for family in this country
to resolve on November 3rd. So while I champion
the Foreign Service, have known demarches,
canapes, as well as rotten tomatoes thrown
at my face after explaining some indefensible
policy, that is the gilded servant's payment
for the bullet proof car swerving past potholes
then whistling along the freshly-paved airport
road to get out of country just in time. Of course
not every diplomat is so lucky. Just look
at the wall of the fallen the next time you meet
a contact at the State Department.

I HEAR

What do you hear?

I am hearing
women turning
in droves, in shoals,
in suburbans.

What do you hear?

I hear countless black
voices whispering
in the longest lines
Atlanta has ever seen.

What do you hear?

I hear millions picking up
phones to talk to you and me,
we surrogates carrying words
from Kamala and Joe.

What do you hear?

I hear myself writing the
departure song of all
pols who are duplicitous,
smooth-talking—except

when mispronouncing
Kamala's and other
brothers' and sisters'
names—ignoring that

Black Lives Matter.

What do you hear?

I hear myself composing
the Inaugural Poem,
the Poem of the first
100 days, the Ode

of the Dream's restoration,
of our Good Name,
of our Signature
to the Climate Accord.

What do you hear?

I hear blue waters licking
pacifically from the West
to the Atlantic. I hear us
marching singing

cleaning house at 1600
Pennsylvania Avenue
and over many many
state houses and dependencies

What do you hear?

I hear the Angel on my left,
God on the side. He pretends
to no color. He cannot stand
His name invoked in vain.

So God, just sit back,
watch us listen to conscience
and draw infinite energy from
its well.

See us go out and retrieve
the game, save the side.
Ride the ferris wheel again,
bury the shame. Build

a World's Fair once more
near Shea Stadium,
by Seattle's Needle,
in Chicago by Lake Superior.

A new age. America open
to the world.

FROM MICHELLE

The invitation arrived in my dream.
Would you join my husband and me
for a meal? His sister will come to town

and she wanted you to meet again after
these more than forty years. After leis at
Honolulu International Center,

the rousing songs, words of great hope
at your graduation, which he attended
at the end of his penultimate year

at Punahou School, followed by
the rest of the story, Law Review,
Senate, Presidency, reducing

the footprint, while you composed
verses in Spanish, French, Creole,
Portuguese, English, these American

tongues, as he walked by the sea wall
in Havana, spoke in Berlin, saved Detroit
and the national economy, celebrated

the digital revolution, assured millions
of Americans health insurance, while
you wrote constantly, squeezing light

from the noonday Sun, the evening Moon.
You can, and will, go on remembering how
these years have not disappeared, the service

in that Charleston church after the murders
when he sang Amazing Grace his voice
cracking, all of our bones cracking,

the Union in apparent disarray but yet
yes we can, yes we can, and now a chance
to say thank you again for his service,

thank you for your poems, thank you God
for this life, the chance to renew old bonds,
remember pick-up basketball games

with mutual friends, remember
Ka Wai Ola, the literary magazine
on which you and he worked one year apart.

Vote: For the 545

545 children separated..*Not in my name*...
Parents still not found...Torn away from
parents...*Not in my name.* In El Paso under
a then-secret program...*Not in my name.*
Before the program became official practice...
The children once numbered a thousand.
Immigrant rights groups have searched for
parents up remote hillsides, in hamlets and
cities, despite Covid, in Mexico,
Central America...*In my name*...545 have
not seen fathers and mothers since June
2017...60 under five when taken
by Border Patrol, by ICE...*Not in my name.*
Thank you Julia Ainsley, Jacob Soboroff
of *NBC News* for your investigation...
In my name...Thank you *New York Times*
for reporting the story...God, I ask you
to stop benign neglect of your wayward
flock, to act on charges of neglect, of cruel
and unusual punishment, of abuse
of minors ...*In my name*...I ask
my government to tell me why we hurt
these children...*In my name.* I ask fellow citizens
to vote the perpetrators out of office...to call
District Attorneys to ask for grand juries,
to prosecute under human rights law, moral law,
to the full extent of all extant laws. *In my name.*

WE ARE GOING TO PENNSYLVANIA AVENUE

We are going down to Pennsylvania Avenue
to 1600 to be precise. We are getting on buses
and trains. We are walking on Rock Creek Trail.

We are taking Ubers and Lyfts to airports.
We are wearing masks. We have washed our hands.
We are going to take planes, all the planes. Special

charter flights. On the way to Washington National,
Washington Dulles, Baltimore International.
We are starting now. Some of us will need time

to secure our homes, to assure that a designated
family member, a friend, a driver, a walker,
a housekeeper, will take care of the cat,

the dog, the birds. We are going
to Pennsylvania Avenue, to 1600 to be exact.
We have got our kids with us too. They are

used to being out of school. And this is
a lesson in life, in hope, in history, my friends.
And some of us will take our pets as well.

Whatever we can manage. We are not making
iron-fisted rules. We are not going to separate
kids from their parents. We are not going to stop

migrants from getting food and shelter. We are not
going to allow our values to be ridden over any more.
Not any more. We are going to Pennsylvania Avenue.

To 1600 to be exact. We accept the invitation from
Kamala and Joe, from neighbors and friends who tell me
that it is we who will determine our destiny, we who will rescue

our Dream. So Kamala, Joe, we have your back and we are in front
of you as well and by your side. We are walking, getting into cars,
trains, buses, planes. We are on our way. And we are not going

to stop on November 3rd. No Sir. No Ma'am. On January 20th
we are going to fill every square inch of the Mall. And
we are not stopping even then. We are going to go back home

renewed, energized, ready to bring the prodigal son,
the prodigal daughter, the prodigal father, the prodigal mother,
back to work, to life, to the dream. *Yes, we will.*

Before the Debate

Joe is going to make us proud tonight. In a blue suit with a blue kerchief
and a deep cry from the heart. He is moving the suburbs. He is turning
heads of unemployed and employed men and women. We are facing
unprecedented razor-thin races in some of the once safely red states.
Texas is tied tonight. Georgia is tied. Florida is tied. Democrats
have the lead in Arizona, Nevada, Pennsylvania, Michigan, Wisconsin.
Ohio is tilting still towards the other guy. Not to worry. We are going
for victory in every state and every dependency. What about Puerto Rico?
What about American citizens of Puerto Rico who are not allowed
to vote? Go figure, America. We need to fix that abomination
in the new administration. We need to manifest equal opportunity
and equal representation. Washington DC is waiting. And we need
to respect judicial precedent as well. We must get the Senate back.
We need the mandate to turn this ship around out of the shoals, away
from the rocks, the triangle, the damned virus swirling into our noses
and mouths. We will Joe. We will phone every single Democrat
in the state of Texas. Thank you Beto for leading that campaign.
And we will join long lines in city after city, Atlanta, Madison,
Chicago, New York. We are not going to stop in a tie. We are not
going to stop with a ballot not posted, not filed. We must take the
country back to Paris to sign that Accord. We must get our farmers
to market in China to trade their grains. We must help to save
the rain forest everywhere. We must breathe, America. And tonight,
as Joe goes, with our prayers, with our hopes, we go, the Dream again
in our hands. And we note that the path for the opponent is narrow
and disappearing. But we will not let up. Go and vote, early if you can,
in person if you can. Go vote. Go Kamala. Go Joe.

A Family Matter

Thank you for reading, your support of
my verses. I am crying happily, dancing

in mind and memory, my blood too, two steps
to the side, one step back, clap. Come back

island. Right now! Let me lick soursop, spoon
avocado flesh on bread, *manje maten*, breakfast

on the table with poems and names, Kenscoff,
la coquille, the idea of a bridge across the sea,

a bicoastal life; but all is well, we are living
in a moment of great hope, at the cusp of

a new world on both sides of the water.
We can only rise, bring family back together,

limit the size of our footprint, and pray
to God to start bothering once more

with the world, to wrest control again
from demons of fire, wind and water.

Rainbow

We are now just hours away.
Your bags have to be packed,
not only with clothes but memories,
books, dedications. They must
also go with blessings. The new life
on the island will be rich. Although
bandits will parade the streets
and interfere with dreams,
they will not be the only drivers
of the polity. Children will smile.
Teachers will open doors
of classes and pupils rise
in chorus singing praise to
the morning light, hope
written in the rainbow. Spirits
for good are walking too
in the same streets, keeping
watch in the neighborhoods.
The island's friends and children
abroad are looking for any
excuse to come back.
The rainbow will protect the
dreams of all. Look up at the
sky after the rain, sun
bursting in primary colors.

IN LOVE AND POLITICS

I miss you now more than I did yesterday and a whole lot more than a month
ago. This accumulating, sometimes leaping, dizzying desire is splendid, grand,
and gives me almost infinite energy, but to where is our train hurtling? Are we
riding in Lawrence's Coney Island of the mind, the America he observed then
a year before I was born, and this America today; when will it fulfill the Dream?
Every Sunday when I go to see my brother I pass a line of cars a few miles long
outside a church on Randolph Road. The drivers wish to satisfy hunger waiting for
them at their homes in this time of virus, lost jobs, not enough money to pay
mortgage or rent. I have read about soup kitchens, the Great Depression, dust,
scrabble, have seen Henry Fonda play Joad in *The Grapes of Wrath*. But to see
ordinary people, hungry now, in automobiles? To see shooting in the back of black
men on grainy police cams, to see George Floyd, his life pressed out. There is
something rotten in America, Shakespeare wrote once about Denmark. There's
something awry in the pigsty, a ferret in the coop, a bandicoot, a rat, a snake.
There is something not right on one side of the debate stage. Yet, there is
enormous hope, belief in the good, and in loving kindness, the man, senator,
widower, his wife killed in a car crash, who rode Amtrak every morning
to Washington, every evening back to Delaware, to join his children for dinner
and to put them to bed. This ordinary, decent Joe, has my vote, and will soon
have a new name and title, extraordinary Joe, extraordinary president. Shall we
take the metro to the Mall, get off at the Smithsonian, walk together to find
a patch of grass, lay down a blanket in our mind, a carousel, a pretzel stand,
then raise our hands in glee on the Ferris wheel reciting poetry on Inauguration Day?

THE OTHER SIDE

Mother reads two poems every night, from *Uncivil War*, a book
I wrote about our bloody island history. She asks what I mean
exactly by tigers? She says she remembers reading about sepalika
flowers. She says she has never understood poetry, but with
a wide-eyed gratitude, innocence, and love for her child,
opens the book, the only one that interrupts her Rosary,
Our Fathers, Hail Marys. I am grateful too, humbled,
to have the chance to live with my mother as she prays
and reads before what's to come, when the book gets
handed on, and the war, with mercy, ends.

TRUTH IN ELEVEN

What say you about
the fleeting passage,
whether you reach
maturity for seven years
or seventy, what
will remain in the mind?
Did you bring light?
Heal a broken heart?
Walk across the bridge
when nobody cared,
cars whistling by?

A MIGRANT STATES

I hope these migrant states feed
your imagination and tranquilize
your heart, that you wake up
emboldened by their coming

of age in America recognizing
you can still remake the life
story, become an other,
an American. So goodbye

old country. See you later,
sweet coconut. I will miss
you blue green sea
at Trincomalee. I belong

now to these multitudes,
whose ancestors formed
first nations, who arrived
chained on dark ships,

whose contemporaries,
breathing free, boarded
jumbo jets, driven by
the promise, or who learned

on the underground railroad,
that we will not allow the dream
to die, that we will walk again
across John Lewis bridge,

on the Mall, in the streets
of cities across the land
until black lives matter
and the dream is realized.

Make it Nude

How many poems have you written?
You must not be very busy in Washington.
— Eduardo

I took these days off. I had to say
goodbye to my life. But don't be
alarmed. Mine is a literary reckoning,
preparation of a will, ritual suicide.
I will rise again light as ash coating

feathers flapping in the still-glowing air
after the bomb, the virus, the curse
of the orange-haired tyrant. America
once more, the dream that stirred my
Allen Ginsberg crazy-wisdom

patriotism, innocence and optimism,
harmonium-winded hallucination.
But I am not Allen Ginsberg.
I have shaved my beard.
Don't be a prude. Make it nude.

LOVE YOUR NEIGHBOR

God gave you a son and daughter,
father and mother, brothers,
a sister. Your parents brought
you up. Now it is your turn
to care for mother in her old
age. And so it shall be when
you too will need your son
and daughter to come and do
the needful, to care for you
when ill and feeble. You are
lucky to have children. What
about those whose kids
have been taken away, shot
in the street, in a foreign land
fighting for some vague motive
in the head of a headless
government? What about those
who have nobody, who must
depend on the village, on a friend?
Let us remember the neighbor.
Let us take care of each other.

VOTE

I am ready to zoom into your classrooms. All you have
to say is "come on down." I am assuming a 50-state and
500-dialect strategy. I don't give a bollocks about the
right way to eat a pork bun or a fried tomato. I will be
the most local candidate adopting the basic rules
taught in the Ten Commandments, in the Koran,
the Talmud, and the Dada Manifesto. Liberty
absolutely. And respect for tradition at the same time.
I will put on the clothes you wish to give me
and change my tune depending on the neighborhood.
I want your vote. And I want everybody else's vote.
I want a mandate multiplied, the mother lode
of mandates. And I am depending on you to catch
the buzz, to remember the civics lessons
of your parents, the example of Martin Luther King
and Martin Luther nailing 95 theses on the doors
of dominion. I will not allow my opponent to engage
in a Southern strategy or a Rust Belt romp. I will show
up in all the unexpected places. Are you waiting for me
in Wichita, in Saint Louis, in the Bayou? Get your
road signs ready in the big country of Montana and
place them in the potato crop of Idaho. I will not
be denied. 100 million people, who did not vote
the last time, are depending on me to get their asses
out of home and to the post office, the polling station.
Do not leave a stone unturned. Honor your God,
your father and mother. Respect your spouse.
And go forth and win this mother, brother, sister.

THE ARTIST'S ROLE

The manufacturer of bonsai takes pride in miniature houses, gardens
and villages. The perfection of details. Doorknob in exact proportion
to the door as in the real life model. Work of a master craftsman.
Mistress of fine inlays. But while the artist labors politicians
are booming in the battle of light against darkness. The Manichean
satisfaction, dual, competing, warring states of the soul laid out
in opposing camps. What role does the miniaturist play?
Will his knobs and latches correspond to the real life models
no matter who wins political power? Can we continue
to make light and gladden hearts while the virus kills
and one gang leader tries to steal the democracy, unmasked?

Preamble

We are starting to roll. We are coming to you
through the internet. And when the weather is right,
masked, we are coming to your door. We will ring
the bell, then step back six feet and wait for you
to pick up the leaflets we have left in your mailbox.
And we will wait for you to open them up and look
over at us and ask, why did you take so long...as you
tell us that you have had your bag packed but
you will not go anywhere except to the ballot box.
Not now. The current occupant has gone too far,
broken every rule and every dream. And we are
going to post them back, on the walls, on columns,
and in the official residence of our dreams, the house
of the people we will rescue at 1600 Pennsylvania Avenue.

NEAR THE RIVER

Let the reggae play, slow and sway, we are
not by the river but we are okay, we will
find friendship in need and bring her water,
serve her wine, outside, even in Rockville,
the town center, a tavern open to evening light,
clinking glasses, unfurling grape leaves,
and we will let the reggae play in our minds,
slow and sway, we are not by the river but
we are okay, under the sky, undressing leaves,
glasses sparkling, saying you can sing of politics
and bringing scoundrels to the river to baptize
and make them God's children. But for now,
let the reggae play, slow and sway. We can't
transform the city in a day. We can't save all
the people all the time, but we can sit down
under the evening sky stripping grape leaves,
clinking glasses of iced wine.

GRIOTS AND ROSES

I listen to Dylan tonight
as I fill in the circle of
my dream. I listen
to Joan Baez tonight
as I fill in the circle
of my hope. I listen
to Leonard Cohen in
his tower of song as I
fill in the circle of the
wrong. I will carry
my circle, filled out,
sealed, to post
tomorrow. I invite
you to make
ceremonies with your
circles and go to the
post office the next
day. Send those
circles into
the heart of the flame.
See them fly unscathed,
turn into rain, sprout and
'shroom in the Rose Garden,
morning in America come.

A Late Revolt

I am a wealthy man. I have two
children—prosperous in mind,
generous in heart—and I am about
to publish my twenty-first book.
I never imagined I would have
so many lyric adventures, so many
loves percolating from fissures
in the earth, and, yes, hopes
derailed as well. But I am sailing,
and of sound mind still, practicing
abstemious eating, preparing
for the longer haul. I invite you
to join me for the rest of the journey.
No more Cyclops. No more sirens.
Just a few shoals in the last stretch
of the bay, a sunken bridge that linked
Bharat once to the island, over which
Hanuman's monkeys marched to rescue
Sita. Yes, Ravana has taken a firm hold
on paradise and minorities have turned
irrelevant in parliament, but seas
are rising and the big powers are
yapping at the borders of the island,
and I am sailing still over the last
few hundred meters, and no patrol boat
has caught me yet, and the state
has no record of what I carry in my hold.

Too Much

I don't think anyone has ever written a book about this,
he tells me, tongue in jowl, but I suspend my disbelief
just long enough falling completely before the joke then
smiling widely and on all sides of my face
and the subject. So, yes I am writing a book about love.
I wrote before about a tsunami and an uncivil war. Now
I write not quite about a tsunami although sadness hits like
a wall of water and I have visited black, bottomless pits
and the edges of ponds that seem like rousing rivers
roaring to a nearby precipitous drop. And I have felt
slings like teargas canisters fogging my eyes and head as
I swig a tumbler of whiskey and peer at the midnight
screen imagining the street scene near the White House,
citizens protesting against murder of black brothers
and sisters as I think of my island love whose heart
is no longer open to nostalgias of the past once
it decided that geography, a couple of bodies of water,
an ocean, and the gulf of age, were too much.

ON EARTH'S MALL

Washington city streets are open and the crowd is streaming
into the Mall, from the metro at Smithsonian, stepping out
of cars, marching in from way west and east, north and south.
Will we reach a million gathered between the Monument and
Congress? And why are we here? And who are we?
Women and children, men on bikes, on rollerblades, girls
in splendid summer dresses, and men in hats, women
in hats, and every migrant under the American sun, jostling
to see, or throwing down blankets on the grass and sand; and
sound systems set up, and crowd pushers and arrangers, and
other signs of some guiding principle, the committee for all
the live aids united, that wants all to go well, to be
ordered and peaceful yet firm against injustice, against killing
of black men and women in their homes and cars,
on the streets. Something has turned too rotten in the fridge,
on the counter top, its stench can no longer be ignored—
the stench of human dreams hunted, lynched, burning.
But we will not set any fires. Not this time. We will wear
ethical, biodegradable cut-outs in our holsters, be better
than metal, plastic explosives, killers. We will ask all cops
to turn in weapons and we will give them roses and carnations.
And we will say also to army and national guard and all
other licensed and unlicensed carriers of arms: join us
and let us pass one million, two million, three million,
three hundred million in all malls and squares of these
United States of America. And let us, at the same time,
embrace malls and squares of Paris and Hong Kong,
Buenos Aires and New Delhi. Let us go everywhere
the crow and the dream flies. Let us say with one planetary
sigh building up into song and cry: Black Lives Matter.

FEELING GOOD, ON THE WAY

I feel feel feel good, yes, thanks to you,
to that smile, the talk, the ritual despite
and because of the limits imposed by the
pandemic, without a choice but to open
the window, without a choice but to
launch verses across to all windows
open throughout this one open window
of a world, without shame, but with all
the right notes, I feel feel feel good
thanks to gems dug up in adversity,
coming together after the murder of
breath to say we will stand together
black and white and we will feel, feel,
feel, good, despite the murder, despite
the several hundred thousand dead of
the virus, despite failure to say goodbye
to the remains of parents, sisters,
brothers incinerated into air and stream
and earth but not from memory. We shall
remember and we shall be purified in
fire and water and make justice, George,
from the virus and the murder, that
whacked you double, and we will count
the beads that matter, say the most
essential verse, that greets the day and
asks whether you have eaten, and if you
have slept through the night, and if not,
talks and consoles until you feel a bit
peckish or sleepy and your body and
mind take up the missing elements
and reconcile and make ready to wake up
refreshed, roaring, out on the other side.

Black

Black Lives Matter. Your life matters. Black Lives
Matter. The Mad Hatter's Life Matters. And his right
to change his name, to wipe the mad prejudice
out of words matters. Black Lives Matter. My life
matters. Black Lives Matter. The squirrel's life matters.
Black Lives Matter. The elephants eat bamboo,
and babies gather round their mothers, and there are
no electric fences or shot guns and there is earth to roam
and there are paths to forge. Black Lives Matter.
The police chief, senator, assemblyman, garbage collector,
teacher and poet and all other professions and creatures
on all arks of the world join the march along 16th Street
in Washington D.C. beside giant yellow letters shouting

      Black Lives Matter.

State of the Union

My cheeks are stubbled, eyes tired, but I have taken stock and
noticed that I have come through this long night. In short,
I am alive. And the day offers the promise of sunlight and a walk
in the woods, which I did not want to push too much, so I strolled
for just a few minutes before coming home again to eat a couple
of bulls' eyes as we call egg yolks in the Sri Lankan isle. Now I am
writing while calling friends, both in the union and out. We will help
each other. When one of us falls the others take on pick-up duty.
The march is long. We are not going to leave anyone behind.

So Help me God

Everybody and everything is going local, food chain, love chain,
burial ground. And migrants are in trouble as they cannot go abroad
or come back, and their philosophers, the globalists, are stuck
behind walls and forced to gather wits and think of a world beyond
the pandemic which will allow again for the best minds to travel
to economic centers, to oil the systems, to make new Americans,
whose parents will long with *saudade* for Mother BRIC while
the children speak contemporary bi-coastal slang, byte language,
gig chat, and hip black talk in speech and dress and tattoos until
Ahmaud Arbery gets killed while jogging, or Botham Jean killed
while her home's invaded, or Michael Brown killed walking back
from the store, and George Floyd, his breath snuffed out by
an arresting boot, and the summer is burning police precincts,
and military police are patrolling American streets, and we
philosophers are wondering about the social contract, and how
to keep the lid on top of a boiling and angry cauldron filled with
black lives discounted, rubbed out, Hispanic lives mowed down
delivering food and stacking groceries, Chinese lives, covid-
tinged, opening fruit stands and one-horse restaurants
on Mott Street, and please, fill in your part of the mosaic,
your migrant history. Please tell us how you want
to accommodate yourselves into the society
in which justice is meted according to privilege,
race, circumstance. So help me God.

NOT BEYOND THIS LINE

Have you noticed this country is burning
he asks me? To be honest, I reply, I have
been avoiding the flames although they are
rising in my city as well. And at home,
I have been coping with my own domestic
fires and I am afraid to step out to see
the rage outside. Writing a poem is
the easiest option, the only one I can
imagine and control. although war is
everywhere, and it is time to raise
our hands and say no, not past this line.

AGAINST WAR

I think about young men and women
who chose to go to war, to fight a dictator,
to protect human rights of their neighbors.
I think about different wars in history, how some
presented such clear choices while others
.raised the question: what are we fighting for?
There is a new world war

at home and abroad right now, and a broad impulse
to join ranks of cavalry riding against mortar and cannon.
There is a new war right now and home fires blaze
in the new industries and sites for R&R.
There is a new war and some of us are showing
off bodies and impulses to harm ourselves
and others, in pools, on beaches,

in gathering *en masse* before the altar,
in these first days of summer. There is
a new war and we are losing when the valiant
who sported their human dominion
come back for a Sunday visit to the parents.
Or maybe the parents and other family
are dead already, and we are living now

a kind of community immunity?
I suspect I am falling for a delusion.
Will you help me get me back on track,
dear reader, with mask, gloves and a sign,
so I can walk to the beach and preach,
we are living in end times, go back
to your homes, wrap your faces and pride.

Vote for the Promised Land

The poet has always been touched
in the head. Best to acknowledge
the condition, and in time,
before the Feds come knocking
at the proverbial door, medical
staff in tow. Everybody knows

the singer sings. Everybody
blows, the poet modifies.
Everybody in your head,
in your head: Get out of bed!
Put on your hat. Take your ID
with you in your blood and Go.

Go. Go. Vote. Vote. Vote
for the soul and gut
and walking the last mile.
Vote for the green and blue
and to save the red. Vote
for the Red, White and Blue.

Vote for Earth seen once more
turning on an ice floe, polar bear
fishing. Vote, friends. We have
come a long way but have not
finished yet. Go vote. Bring
your neighbors and friends

to the polls Let us go
down to gym, to school,
to refurbished parking lot.
We have a dream to get on
the road again. Go friends.
Bring me along with you

to the promised land.

GEORGIA ON MY MIND, FOREVER

Jimmy Carter is walking proud today
in the fields of Plains. Stacey Abrams
is working the phones in Atlanta.
Librarians in charge of all public and private
book collections are dusting off studies
that examine FDR's triumph in the state,
Jimmy Carter's presidential victory,
and Bill Clinton, new young pol, how
he squeezed by in 1992. Now, in 2020
Joe Biden is bringing back the bacon and
the greens and the Dream, breaking down
that bloody wall between Red and Blue.
One country. One dream. Georgia
you are making us feel a shiver in our spine,
a song bursting forth from our lungs.
Ray Charles in the state capitol in 1979,
at the piano, an old song for the new South,

Georgia On My Mind.

OWNER, SLAVE, SUBALTERN

for Kamala

Kamala is a distant cousin,
grandfather Gopalan from
Painganadu in Tamil Nadu.

Her father's ancestor,
Hamilton Brown, Irishman,
slave owner in Jamaica, slept

with an unknown woman, almost
certainly a slave, brought from the
West Coast of Africa,

shackled, through the Middle Passage.
In Kamala's roots rights trampled,
consideration as three fifths of a man

and two fifths more of another.
Her Tamil grandfather, subaltern
in British administration, moved

to a post in Chennai. We know
Donald Harris moved to Berkeley
to study for a PhD in economics,

where he met fellow student,
scientist, Shyamala Gopalan,
resulting in Kamala's birth. Kamala

will now serve as Vice President
of the United States, which
I represent as a diplomat, migration

and the Dream realized.
How can I not write about this?
I am proud that one of my people

will be chief advisor, and next
in line, to the president of
this multicultural America.

I am not ashamed to refer
to dark chapters in the story,
in this new age of truth telling,

which makes us stronger, going
ahead towards the Dream wearing
all our colors on our body, in our mind.

To Oz and Beyond

You must be depressed, Mr. President
watching the drip drip of tabulating,
red wall crumbling, and all the king's
men turning mum, just your sons
and personal lawyer braying on Twitter,
and yes, an army of a thousand others
bringing spurious charges before
what was to have been your last line
of defense, the federal and supreme courts.
But your plans were stymied by
the electoral calendar, this unfortunate
need to be reviewed by the people
every four years. Just not enough time
to seal the borders of justice and democracy,
to gut the civic dreams even of your own party
members. Depressing and certainly cheering
to your opponent, that sleepy fellow who
has crawled over the finishing line
with pride while you founder somewhere
in the attic of that now windy mansion,
wondering whether the last ride will come
from a helicopter out and above the Potomac
on the way to Andrews and the final flight
to Mar-a-Lago, then after a swift packing
of bags, by private jet to some territory
in the back of yonder, Oz, beyond.

From Pennsylvania to the Current Resident of 1600 Pennsylvania Avenue

What did you think, Mr President,
that you could hold on against a son of Scranton,
a former senator from neighboring Delaware who
kept in touch with his home town and state,
who was considered Pennsylvania's third senator?
Did you think the former Vice President would
not spend the last day of his campaign visiting
the house where he grew up? What did you think
as you rallied and rallied spreading red hats
everywhere? Did you note that the state's colors
are blue and gold, that its song rails against
tyranny, *'til the bell of independence
filled the countryside*?

The bell is tolling now, Mr President.
Your opponent's numbers are rising as every
vote is counted. We don't need to revisit
the War of Independence. You have been, yes,
trumped. but you are free to go back
to your tower. You will be safe there. Americans
respect property rights, although you will understand
if some shout that you have been fired. Not me,
Mr. President, I won't crow. The presidency needs
to show respect and to be respected in turn.
Goodbye. Go with God. Take care of your family.
Have a rest. Go to China if you wish.
Or Europe. You are free.

New, New Deal

We will take the high road, and the low road as well. We are not going
to let the demon slip, slide and rear back to strike. No, Sir. No, Ma'am.
Now is the time to say no more water or blood will flow under this door.

No more excuses. No more reflection that he too heads a family, with sons
and daughters; is married to a beauty from a foreign land. We are glad
for him as we respect all life. But he did not play his part. He came out

lying and screaming. He broke the contract. He broke our trust. We cannot
stand by as the child is separated from mother and father at the door
to our country. We cannot keep quiet when the black man, running from

a cop, is shot in the back. We cannot allow the future to be snuffed by a
boot pressed to a man's neck. But the killer is out on bail I hear you
laughing. And the one who shall not be named, turning into toast, rhubarb

rash on forehead, red cap with the verb to make and the noun America
on his head—how will he react, aggrieved, bruised, fuming, screaming
in the people's house as the counting turns against him? Will he set the house

on fire? Will the National Guard come to his rescue? Will his team of doctors
from Walter Reed Hospital return for a house call and drag him out to give
something, anything, vital back? Some plasma for the next patient dying

in the ICU? Will he release his taxes now? Will he say, I am sorry for raising
the profile of the alt-right, for saying QAnon is okay, for shutting the door on
refugees, for inviting dictators to drink coffee and eat apple pie?

This poem has become a reality shindig, a public bloodletting. Yet I will
take high and low roads. I said so at the beginning. I say it again. Play it Sam.
Play it in Nebraska, Iowa, California, Hawaii. I will not follow

in his footsteps. I am ready to serve you who voted for me and you
who did not. That is my gift back to Scranton, to Wilmington, to all
who have joined the American team for a New, New Deal.

BETWEEN GREAT FEAR, GREAT HOPE

Owners are boarding up throughout the city,
small, big shops, whole malls, as if preparing
for a hurricane, a sea swell, a storm surge,
that wood will protect glass and stock,
while shutters go up at home and nobody
steps out except also to vote before
scurrying back to sit out the night where
fears of crystal shattering are filling daymares
in this once blessed land smarting from
four years of locusts, plague. Yet, voting
remains the last chance to sandbag
ship, house, store from the curse, the storm,
power station left live in the middle of the field
near pine tree forests by beetles brushed,
offering wood cheap, on the dollar,
to shop owners, a fire sale, late extraction
of profit, an election to end all elections,
or to begin them again, Contract Renewed.

Texas (for Beto)

Powered by People will not roll over, Texas.
Powered by People will keep knocking
on doors, texting, calling on the phone
with news of the community, of food banks
opening, of the next jobs fair. And, in some
not so distant future, the Lone Star state

will reduce the speed limit on its highways,
and rulers with silver spoons in their mouths
will come down from observing rigs
and slaughterhouses. No state belongs
to one party or the other. Voting is personal
like the beloved you choose to receive the letter

that reveals your soul. We will build
the republic of Texas, the democratic
republic of migrants, old families,
grandchildren of pioneers, under
an enormous tent the size of Texas.
We will not give up the permanent campaign

to turn the state house blue, to win a senate seat
or two, to deliver one day in the future for
the Democratic presidential candidate, born here,
or elsewhere, in the union. No more red and blue
divide, despite appearances, despite harassment
of the Biden bus on the highway. There will always be

two sides to an argument, or three or four. Let people
know options. Register a Texan every day, break bread
and share it. In the privacy of the booth, the
new voter will decide. And we will respect
the decision even if it hurts tonight that Texas
did not turn blue by six percentage points.

THE DAY AFTER

It does not matter if you can't call.
We have much to talk about and
we will catch up, the room

in the heart reserved, the key
in the mind. Just think. The door
will open. Just think the dance

will continue. On Saturday
November 7th I saw the message
slide across my computer screen,

and I leaped for joy, found
my mother, tears falling down.
You were in class but had

heard the news, exclamation points
ringing through the phone, and then
in the city hundreds,

thousands gathering
in Black Lives Matter Plaza
popping champagne, grooving

to the free beat, free at last. Now,
the day after, euphoria just keeps
growing, learning about Kamala's

Tamil roots, Joe's love of Irish
poetry. This is a couple to invite
for Thanksgiving, to say grace

despite the virus and the dying.
They know exactly what to do.
Look at their four priorities.

Covid, the economy,
racial equity, climate change.
Brilliant. Heartbreaking.

We are being guided
by intelligent trade winds,
all our prayers rising.

(The Mother of)...Pandemics

NOTES FOR THE DAYS AFTER

I will not allow the virus to seep into every conversation,
every glance out of the window, every reading of the news.
And it would be most unseemly to publish an entire book
of Covid poems even if I have written a rather large number.
I will clean the inbox, throw some into the bin. Yes, there are

poets defined by circumstances beyond their own small steps.
Owen's *Anthem for Doomed Youth* foretold his demise
and the end of a generation. But the human race survived.
Now there are many asymptomatic carriers and untouched
ones. And there are already a lot of dead and a lot more

emotionally scarred. And yes, hotels on my paradise island
will become vast halls for visits by wind and elephants.
Or the sea. Every grand illusion gets its tsunami one day.
That is the fatalist's view. It has not been contradicted.
Look at how swiftly the virus has changed our culture,

our ways of greeting, our decoupling. But after the war
has ended, after we have put this quarantine into a back
pocket in our collective mind, we will venture out again
into the forever-changed world to see who is moving
about, who has come out of the dark night, alive.

FEAR

I am afraid that the island
no longer belongs to me,
and my waist will never deflate,
the hair on my head not return,
and the dictator will give
his power to his son, and
my daughter not know
the land of her father,
and that you will remain
in your neighborhood
to wait for a new suitor.
I am afraid of life
after the pandemic.

MURDER MOST FOUL (IN THE TRENCHES OF COVID-19)

The griot is telling the story of our dream smashed on the seat of the cadillac
in Dallas: President Kennedy mowed down in his prime, a *Murder most foul.*

I listen to the song day and night. It is wise, foreboding, precise. It remembers
the early days of movies, the flowering of jazz, and the Beatles about to arrive

to hold our hands. It goes into the future, the past, and it warns that Kennedy,
shot like a dog in broad daylight, in the street, is only the first: Malcom, Martin,

Robert will also fall. And though the song does not mention this, John Lennon
as well. The song ends and it begins again, like a wave breaking, receding,

then coming back strong. a tsunami. As a musical piece, it lasts for twenty
minutes. In my mind it does not end, like a dark cloak I wear at the wake,

that began in 1963, the year between *Lady Chatterly's Lover* and the Beatles'
first LP in Larkin's poem about sexuality, a little too late for him he said,

a dark cloak I wear in my mind as I think about the magic bullet
like the one that killed Rabin and the peace accord with Palestine,

like the murder most foul of Vijaya, Neelan and Lasantha, peacemakers
at home, victims of murder most foul, environmental crimes, oil spills,

murders of activists, how they fog up the atmosphere like the nuclear cloud
in Ray Davies' Apeman, I think I cannot undress, Bob Dylan. Not until

we reclaim the civil space on Pennsylvania Avenue, not until we refurbish
the ploughshare before the United Nations, not until we unravel Covid-19.

Beat / Bat / Frappe

Beat the drum with the hands
of the heart. Beat the drum
with the hands of the mind.
Beat the drum with the hands

of God. Beat the drum
with the spirit inside. Beat
the drum without stopping.
Beat the drum until the end

of life and after we enter
the earth. Beat, beat, beat,
beat, beat the drum. Beat
the drum with the spirit

of God in hand, in drum,
in memory. When
the drum beats, I am
with you. We are one.

THE NEW AEROPLANES

In this AC world even countries like Kazakhstan
are no more remote than Canada or Mexico.
A friend in Manhattan sees clear skies, across
the East River, over Kennedy. I write from
Washington D.C. Commuters to the odd
federal office open still look over the Potomac
to Reagan Airport and spy, bemused, lines
of Canada Geese flying in formation. They
are able to travel old routes unhindered,
celebrating the suddenly open skies.

TOPPLING

Give me your elbow. Take the Host in your hands;
but, Man, the Pope just spoke the sermon
from his living room, on video tape. This matter
is turning extreme. A taxi driver got infected
from his ride. Can we really shut down a city,
a region, the whole world? Be prepared
we are told. We were waiting for fire, a bomb,
icebergs breaking up in our soup; but this virus
is more insidious, a slow shaking and swaying
of the building in the mind before it falls.

Sheltering in Place with Your Poem, Susana Case

—A good poem for its time, but now, none of us should let strangers into our homes. Glad that nothing happened to you.
—A comment posted on FB

I am lifting up my hands in the general direction of Heaven,
stones in my palms. Must I carry my fellow man or woman?
May I just arrange for myself and immediate family? How
will I, or you, dear poet—who wrote the original *Sheltering*—
change even one bigot let alone a few million, and they are
scattered throughout the globe. Go home Chinese virus. Get
thee behind closed doors, Central American fruit picker,
and God forbid, you will allow Spanish-speaking, Creole-
warbling, Arabic-moaning handymen into your private
bathroom to fix a ceramic wall and a shower head?
Have you lost your marbles? Strangers in the sacred
space of your toilet? Thank God, the co-op board
stepped in and corrected this utopian fantasy.
Thank God you are alive and I am too. As for
the handymen, well, it is a free country still and
they can go in search of the American dream, across
to the borderlands and beyond, so help them God.

View from the Bedroom

The view from my house is grey,
sky clouded, cold wind blowing
through a crack in the picture window,

but evidence abounds that spring
is about to open, pink and white
buds on cherry trees, which

my mother fertilized every year
and which bore a hundred pounds
in slightly tart fruit—not these days,

the garden allowed to go
to seed naturally by a self-
declared, benign and absent

poet in quarantine staring
at the computer screen,
and beyond, Spring turning.

LATE NIGHT OLIVE OIL

Let us put the letters and fears and boiling emotions on the page. Mummy,
why did you go to the kitchen, stealthily without a word to your sleeping
son? Without your walker? To find the large bottle of olive oil. To pour
it on the table and floor, to fill a small vessel which you meant to carry
back to your room as if nobody would notice until you called my name
because you could not negotiate the rest of the way from dining table
to bedroom, vessel in hand, without cane or walker. I write to atone
for my flailing words saying, never, never, never again. The kitchen
is prohibited. Your mania for oil in the hair is prohibited. The stealthy,
mischievous childish, truant foray into the darkness with a torch
in hand, which you forgot on the countertop—all of this is prohibited.
Your losing memory and control are prohibited. These words
are prohibited. Decline and death are prohibited.

The Lesson

What would José Emilio say if I was to show up this morning
at his home on Avenida Progreso, to eat some red-yolked eggs
 and chat about the sand falling in the hour glass, the beauty
of a few rivers? Or my dearest Yeats? Shall I stroll with him

along Fleet Street to spy a shop window with a fountain
and a bobbing ball, bobbing on its way to Innisfree, to that
small house of clay and wattles made? Shall I offer
Tom Sterns Eliot a peach? We sit in a cafe on a cobble-

stoned Boston street, and the yellow fog is rubbing its muzzle
on the windowpane. Shall I pop over to Dulles, ask for
a seat on the first flight once flights resume, saying
I would like to land again in Heathrow where my adventure

in the West began? Who did I read right off the tarmac?
Thomas Hardy, Dylan Thomas, *A Shropshire Lad?*
The Prelude and T*he Charge of the Light Brigade?*
Who turned my heart to a quiver, tears pouring down

cheeks as Othello, naive, foolish, fell for Iago's trap,
and killed Desdemona, his beloved. Killed. Murder
most foul. Did he deserve to end it all? Did Shakespeare
have any other ruse available to finish his tragedy

to our satisfaction? Would we accept solitary confinement,
parole after five years for the Moor? Forgiveness is a tough
field to hoe. Death will take the noble and the weak,
scoundrels and saints. But the grand old verses will survive

as long as we live, pottering about the house, confined,
Covid raging outside. I am lucky I have not been blinded,
or run out to the moor, hoodwinked by my own daughters.
I am lucky to have lived, and to have loved, and all that jazz.

I am lucky to have a son and a daughter, to have helped them
grow, to see their drawings on my heart. I am lucky to have
shared the house with my mother again these last few years
and pray that she will stay strong and go only when she is ready.

I am lucky that what I have learned I teach, these lines my class.

TORCH

The flame may seem fragile,
small, almost nothing at all,
but as you carry it from room

to room in the dark, the bobbing,
flickering wick lights up mind
and heart and gives hope.

And the Sun is waiting
around the corner of morning,
to come on stage, to rise.

Blues, Quarantine

Why this quarantine do I drink scotch
with my screen? Why wear a sarong

from morning to evening? Why
let my beard sprout white stubble

like bushes sprinkled with first snow?
Why make beauty of a dalliance

that might have been, may still be,
a long-term building? Why ask

questions that have no answers?
Why ask questions? Why not just

be, see, hear, touch, feel without
any extraneous pondering?

THE WALK

I must trust us, know that you are there, that we are together,
that we are going to be patient and confront this plague
and conquer it with intelligence, faith and compromise,
that destiny leads us, and the future will flourish again
with flowers carried in the hand, from my house
to yours, as in that Saturday when I dropped the rules
of my work and walked in the open air, to visit the florist
in the square by the church, before continuing my way to
look for you in your neighborhood, before the curious
stares of neighbors, this gentleman whom we have seen
seated in an armored sedan, who walks on the street,
a common man, a human being, roses in hand.

THE CANDLE (MIGRATORY BIRD)

I must tell you that I am lighting a candle in my mind
and I beg that the flame lasts through the night, that it will
not be put out by a man, too afraid, mad, young in thought.
Let us embrace the darkness and accept each other's
absolute freedom to fly to the other end of the earth
to discover that the world is round and love has no choice—
the migratory route already drawn—but to return, to return.

About the Author

Indran Amirthanayagam (www.indranmx.com) writes in English, Spanish, French, Portuguese and Haitian Creole. He has published twenty-one poetry books, including *Blue Window* (translated by Jennifer Rathbun), *The Migrant States*, *Coconuts on Mars*, *The Elephants of Reckoning* (winner 1994 Paterson Poetry Prize), *Uncivil War*, and *The Splintered Face: Tsunami Poems*. In music, he recorded *Rankont Dout*. He edits the *Beltway Poetry Quarterly* (www.beltwaypoetry.com); curates www.ablucionistas.com; writes https://indranamirthanayagam.blogspot.com; co-directs Poets & Writers Studio International; writes a weekly poem for *Haiti en Marche* and *El Acento*; and hosts *The Poetry Channel* (https://youtube.com/user/indranam). He has received fellowships from the Foundation for the Contemporary Arts, the New York Foundation for the Arts, The US/Mexico Fund for Culture, and the Macdowell Colony. He is a 2021 Emergent Seed grant winner. New books, including *Powèt nan po la* (*Poet of the Port*) and *Isleño*, will be published in late 2021 and early 2022.